The Daily Turkish Challenge

Learn 10 Turkish Words a Day for 7 Weeks

Introduction

📖 Welcome to "Learn 10 Turkish Words a Day for 7 Weeks"! This book is designed to provide an engaging and effective learning experience for children 👶 and beginners who are eager to discover the beauty of the Turkish language 🇹🇷. With its carefully curated selection of words and interactive approach, this book aims to make language learning a fun 🎨 and enjoyable journey.

Learning a new language can be both exciting 😀 and challenging 😔, but fear not! We have crafted this book 📖 with your learning needs in mind. Each day, you will encounter a set of ten Turkish words that are carefully chosen to be useful and practical in everyday situations. These words cover various themes 🌳🏛️🍴, allowing you to expand your vocabulary and gain confidence in your language skills 🗣️.

To facilitate your learning process, we have provided corresponding English words 🇬🇧 alongside the Turkish words, allowing you to establish meaningful connections between the two languages. By actively engaging in writing ✍️ down (4x) the correct Turkish words, you will reinforce your memory and develop a solid foundation in the language. Embrace the joy of discovery as you unlock 🔓 new words each day, steadily building your language skills one step at a time.

This book is meant to be your companion 📖 throughout the course of seven weeks, providing you with a structured learning experience. Each week is carefully planned to introduce new vocabulary [NEW] while reinforcing previously learned words, allowing you to review and consolidate your knowledge. Make sure to allocate a few minutes 🕐 each day to engage with the exercises and activities provided. Consistency is key 🔑, and your dedication will yield rewarding results 🏆.

Whether you are a young language enthusiast or a curious beginner, this book is designed to cater to your needs. The vibrant illustrations 🎨 and interactive exercises are intended to spark your imagination and keep you engaged. Remember, learning a language should be an enjoyable experience, and we hope this book will ignite 🔥 your passion for Turkish.

As you embark on this language learning adventure, we encourage you to embrace the challenge 🏁, celebrate your progress 🎉, and have fun along the way. Learning 10 Turkish words a day is an achievable goal 🎯, and with perseverance and dedication, you will unlock the doors 🚪 to a new world of communication and understanding.

Happy learning! 🌼

Table of Contents

Week 1

Day 1: Numbers

One	Bir (beer)
Two	İki (ee-kee)
Three	Üç (ewch)
Four	Dört (duhrt)
Five	Beş (besh)
Six	Altı (ahl-tee)
Seven	Yedi (yeh-dee)
Eight	Sekiz (seh-keez)
Nine	Dokuz (doh-kooz)
Ten	On (ohn)

Write the right words down twice on the next page

Six	....	....
Two	....	....
Eight	....	....
Four	....	....
Five	....	....
Eight	....	....
Seven	....	....
Three	....	....
Nine	....	....
Ten	....	....
One	....	....
Two	....	....
Ten	....	....
Four	....	....
Five	....	....
Six	....	....
Seven	....	....
Three	....	....
Nine	....	....
One	....	....

Week 1

Day 2: Colors

Red	Kırmızı (kur-muh-zuh)
Blue	Mavi (mah-vee)
Yellow	Sarı (sah-ruh)
Green	Yeşil (yeh-sheel)
Orange	Turuncu (too-roon-joo)
Purple	Mor (moor)
Pink	Pembe (pem-beh)
Black	Siyah (see-yah)
White	Beyaz (bey-ahz)
Gray	Gri (gree)

Write the right words down twice on the next page

Red	....	....
Purple	....	....
White	....	....
Gray	....	....
Orange	....	....
Purple	....	....
Blue	....	....
Black	....	....
White	....	....
Gray	....	....
Pink	....	....
Blue	....	....
Yellow	....	....
Green	....	....
Orange	....	....
Pink	....	....
Red	....	....
Black	....	....
Yellow	....	....
Green	....	....

Week 1

Day 3: Family

Mother	Anne (ahn-neh)
Father	Baba (bah-bah)
Brother	Erkek kardeş (ehr-kehk kahr-desh)
Sister	Kız kardeş (kuz kahr-desh)
Son	Oğul (o-ool)
Daughter	Kız evlat (kuz ev-lat)
Grandfather	Dede (deh-deh)
Grandmother	Babaanne (bah-bah-ahn-neh)
Uncle	Amca (ahm-jah)
Aunt	Hala (hah-lah)

Write the right words down twice on the next page

Aunt	....	....
Father	....	....
Mother	....	....
Uncle	....	....
Brother	....	....
Sister	....	....
Son	....	....
Daughter	....	....
Grandfather	....	....
Sister	....	....
Aunt	....	....
Grandmother	....	....
Uncle	....	....
Son	....	....
Grandmother	....	....
Father	....	....
Brother	....	....
Daughter	....	....
Grandfather	....	....
Mother	....	....

Week 1

Day 4: Food

Bread	Ekmek (ek-mek)
Rice	Pirinç (pee-rinch)
Meat	Et (et)
Vegetables	Sebzeler (seb-zeh-ler)
Fruit	Meyve (may-veh)
Milk	Süt (soot)
Cheese	Peynir (pay-neer)
Eggs	Yumurta (yoo-moor-tah)
Soup	Çorba (chor-bah)
Dessert	Tatlı (taht-luh)

Write the right words down twice on the next page

Cheese ....

Meat ....

Dessert ....

Vegetables ....

Fruit ....

Milk ....

Vegetables ....

Eggs ....

Soup ....

Dessert ....

Bread ....

Rice ....

Meat ....

Fruit ....

Milk ....

Cheese ....

Bread ....

Eggs ....

Soup ....

Rice ....

Week 1

Day 5: Animals

Dog	Köpek (koe-pek)
Cat	Kedi (keh-dee)
Lion	Aslan (ahs-lahn)
Sheep	Koyun (koy-oon)
Pig	Domuz (doh-mooz)
Monkey	Maymun (may-moon)
Tiger	Kaplan (kahp-lahn)
Bear	Ayı (ah-yuh)
Horse	At (aht)
Bird	Kuş (koosh)

Write the right words down twice on the next page

Monkey	....	....
Cat	....	....
Bird	....	....
Lion	....	....
Sheep	....	....
Pig	....	....
Monkey	....	....
Tiger	....	....
Bear	....	....
Horse	....	....
Bird	....	....
Dog	....	....
Cat	....	....
Lion	....	....
Sheep	....	....
Pig	....	....
Horse	....	....
Tiger	....	....
Bear	....	....
Dog	....	....

Week 1

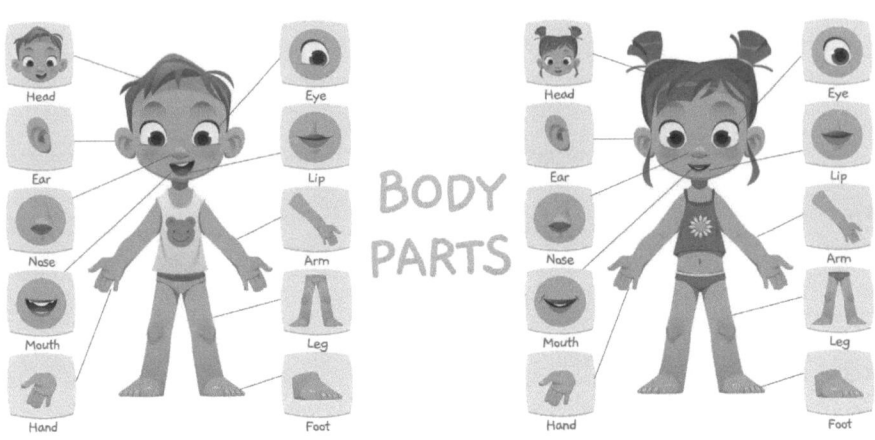

Day 6: Body

Head	Baş (bash)
Neck	Boyun (boy-oon)
Belly	Karn (kahrn)
Shoulder	Omuz (oh-mooz)
Knee	Diz (diz)
Back	Sırt (suhr-t)
Arms	Kollar (kol-lahr)
Hands	Eller (el-ler)
Legs	Bacaklar (bah-chak-lar)
Feet	Ayaklar (ah-yahk-lar)

Write the right words down twice on the next page

Shoulder	....	....
Back	....	....
Feet	....	....
Belly	....	....
Hands	....	....
Shoulder	....	....
Knee	....	....
Back	....	....
Arms	....	....
Hands	....	....
Neck	....	....
Feet	....	....
Head	....	....
Neck	....	....
Belly	....	....
Knee	....	....
Legs	....	....
Arms	....	....
Head	....	....
Legs	....	....

Week 1

Day 7: Weather

Sun	Güneş (goo-nesh)
Rain	Yağmur (yah-moor)
Cloud	Bulut (boo-loot)
Wind	Rüzgar (ruez-gahr)
Snow	Kar (kahr)
Thunder	Gök gürültüsü (gohk goo-rool-too-soo)
Lightning	Şimşek (shim-shek)
Storm	Fırtına (fur-tee-nah)
Fog	Sis (sis)
Rainbow	Gökkuşağı (gohk-koo-shah-uh)

Write the right words down twice on the next page

Storm	....	....
Rain	....	....
Fog	....	....
Snow	....	....
Cloud	....	....
Wind	....	....
Snow	....	....
Thunder	....	....
Rain	....	....
Lightning	....	....
Storm	....	....
Fog	....	....
Rainbow	....	....
Sun	....	....
Cloud	....	....
Wind	....	....
Thunder	....	....
Lightning	....	....
Rainbow	....	....
Sun	....	....

Week 2

Day 8: Months

January	Ocak (oh-jahk)
February	Şubat (shoo-baht)
March	Mart (mart)
April	Nisan (nee-sahn)
May	Mayıs (mah-yush)
June	Haziran (hah-zee-rahn)
July	Temmuz (teh-mooz)
August	Ağustos (ah-oos-tohs)
September	Eylül (ey-lool)
October	Ekim (eh-kim)

Write the right words down twice on the next page

October	....	....
February	....	....
August	....	....
October	....	....
April	....	....
May	....	....
June	....	....
August	....	....
March	....	....
September	....	....
May	....	....
January	....	....
July	....	....
March	....	....
April	....	....
June	....	....
January	....	....
July	....	....
February	....	....
September	....	....

Week 2

Day 9: School

Teacher	Öğretmen (oe-gret-men)
Student	Öğrenci (oe-gren-jee)
Classroom	Sınıf (suh-nuhf)
Book	Kitap (kee-tahp)
Pen	Kalem (kah-lem)
Pencil	Kurşun kalem (koor-shoon kah-lem)
Desk	Sıra (suh-rah)
Chair	Sandalye (sahn-dah-lyeh)
Homework	Ev ödevi (ev oh-deh-vee)
Exam	Sınav (suh-nav)

Write the right words down twice on the next page

Chair	....	....
Homework	....	....
Teacher	....	....
Student	....	....
Classroom	....	....
Exam	....	....
Pen	....	....
Pencil	....	....
Desk	....	....
Classroom	....	....
Homework	....	....
Exam	....	....
Teacher	....	....
Student	....	....
Desk	....	....
Book	....	....
Pen	....	....
Pencil	....	....
Chair	....	....
Book	....	....

Week 2

Day 10: Transportation

Car	Araba (ah-rah-bah)
Bus	Otobüs (oh-toh-boos)
Train	Tren (tren)
Bicycle	Bisiklet (bee-sik-let)
Motorcycle	Motorsiklet (motor-sik-let)
Boat	Tekne (tehk-neh)
Airplane	Uçak (oo-chahk)
Helicopter	Helikopter (heh-lee-kop-ter)
Truck	Kamyon (kah-myohn)
Metro	Metro (meh-troh)

Write the right words down twice on the next page

Airplane	....	....
Bus	....	....
Train	....	....
Metro	....	....
Truck	....	....
Motorcycle	....	....
Boat	....	....
Airplane	....	....
Helicopter	....	....
Truck	....	....
Metro	....	....
Car	....	....
Bus	....	....
Train	....	....
Bicycle	....	....
Helicopter	....	....
Motorcycle	....	....
Boat	....	....
Bicycle	....	....
Car	....	....

Week 2

Day 11: Clothing

Shirt	Gömlek (goem-lek)
Pants	Pantolon (pahn-toh-lon)
Dress	Elbise (el-bee-seh)
Skirt	Etek (eh-tek)
Jacket	Ceket (jeh-ket)
Shoes	Ayakkabı (ah-yahk-kah-bee)
Socks	Çorap (chor-ap)
Hat	Şapka (shap-kah)
Gloves	Eldiven (el-dee-ven)
Scarf	Atkı (aht-kuh)

Write the right words down twice on the next page

Socks	....	....
Pants	....	....
Dress	....	....
Jacket	....	....
Skirt	....	....
Scarf	....	....
Shoes	....	....
Socks	....	....
Hat	....	....
Gloves	....	....
Scarf	....	....
Shirt	....	....
Pants	....	....
Dress	....	....
Skirt	....	....
Jacket	....	....
Shoes	....	....
Gloves	....	....
Hat	....	....
Shirt	....	....

Week 2

Day 12: Emotions

Happy	Mutlu (moot-loo)
Sad	Üzgün (uez-goon)
Angry	Kızgın (kuz-goon)
Excited	Heyecanlı (hay-eh-jahn-luh)
Surprised	Şaşırmış (sha-suur-muhsh)
Scared	Korkmuş (kor-moosh)
Nervous	Gergin (gehrgin)
Bored	Sıkılmış (suh-kool-muhsh)
Confused	Şaşkın (shash-kun)
Calm	Sakin (sah-kin)

Write the right words down twice on the next page

Confused	....	....
Happy	....	....
Calm	....	....
Surprised	....	....
Sad	....	....
Angry	....	....
Excited	....	....
Nervous	....	....
Scared	....	....
Nervous	....	....
Bored	....	....
Scared	....	....
Calm	....	....
Happy	....	....
Sad	....	....
Bored	....	....
Angry	....	....
Excited	....	....
Surprised	....	....
Confused	....	....

Week 2

Day 13: Hobbies

Reading	Okuma (oh-koo-mah)
Painting	Resim yapma (reh-seem yahp-mah)
Singing	Şarkı söyleme (shar-kuh sooy-leh-meh)
Dancing	Dans etme (dahns et-meh)
Cooking	Yemek pişirme (yeh-mek pee-sheer-meh)
Photography	Fotoğraf çekme (foh-toh-rahf chehk-meh)
Sleeping	Uyuma (oo-yoo-mah)
Writing	Yazma (yahz-mah)
Gardening	Bahçe işleriyle uğraşma (bah-cheh ish-leh-ree-le oo-rahsh-mah)
Sports	Spor (spor)

Write the right words down twice on the next page

Gardening	....	....
Painting	....	....
Photography	....	....
Painting	....	....
Dancing	....	....
Cooking	....	....
Photography	....	....
Sports	....	....
Writing	....	....
Gardening	....	....
Sports	....	....
Reading	....	....
Sleeping	....	....
Singing	....	....
Dancing	....	....
Cooking	....	....
Singing	....	....
Sleeping	....	....
Writing	....	....
Reading	....	....

Week 2

Day 14: Sports

Football	Futbol (foot-bol)
Basketball	Basketbol (bahs-ket-bol)
Tennis	Tenis (teh-nis)
Swimming	Yüzme (yuz-meh)
Volleyball	Voleybol (vo-lay-bol)
Golf	Golf (golf)
Cycling	Bisiklet sürme (bee-sik-let soor-meh)
Running	Koşma (kosh-mah)
Fitness	Fitness (fitness - as in English)
Martial arts	Dövüş sanatları (duh-vuhsh sah-naht-lah-ruh)

Write the right words down twice on the next page

Swimming	....	....
Football	....	....
Fitness	....	....
Basketball	....	....
Golf	....	....
Swimming	....	....
Volleyball	....	....
Golf	....	....
Running	....	....
Cycling	....	....
Running	....	....
Fitness	....	....
Martial arts	....	....
Football	....	....
Basketball	....	....
Tennis	....	....
Martial arts	....	....
Volleyball	....	....
Cycling	....	....
Tennis	....	....

Week 3

Day 15: Nature

Tree	Ağaç (ah-ahch)
Flower	Çiçek (chee-chek)
River	Nehir (neh-heer)
Mountain	Dağ (dah)
Lake	Göl (goel)
Beach	Plaj (plahj)
Forest	Orman (or-mahn)
Grass	Çim (chim)
Star	Yıldız (yuhl-duhz)
Cloud	Bulut (boo-loot)

Write the right words down twice on the next page

Grass	....	....
Beach	....	....
Mountain	....	....
Cloud	....	....
Flower	....	....
River	....	....
Mountain	....	....
Lake	....	....
Beach	....	....
Forest	....	....
Grass	....	....
Star	....	....
Forest	....	....
Cloud	....	....
Tree	....	....
Flower	....	....
River	....	....
Star	....	....
Lake	....	....
Tree	....	....

Week 3

Day 16: Days of the Week

Monday	Pazartesi (pah-zar-teh-see)
Tuesday	Salı (sah-luh)
Wednesday	Çarşamba (char-sham-bah)
Thursday	Perşembe (per-shem-beh)
Friday	Cuma (joo-mah)
Saturday	Cumartesi (joo-mar-teh-see)
Sunday	Pazar (pah-zar)
Yesterday	Dün (duen)
Tomorrow	Yarın (yar-uhn)
Today	Bugün (boo-guen)

Write the right words down twice on the next page

Sunday	....	....
Tuesday	....	....
Saturday	....	....
Today	....	....
Wednesday	....	....
Tomorrow	....	....
Friday	....	....
Saturday	....	....
Yesterday	....	....
Tomorrow	....	....
Today	....	....
Monday	....	....
Thursday	....	....
Wednesday	....	....
Thursday	....	....
Friday	....	....
Monday	....	....
Sunday	....	....
Yesterday	....	....
Tuesday	....	....

Week 3

Day 17: Music

Song	Şarkı (shar-kuh)
Melody	Melodi (meh-lo-dee)
Rhythm	Ritim (ree-teem)
Instrument	Enstrüman (en-stroo-man)
Singing	Şarkı söyleme (shar-kuh sooy-leh-meh)
Band	Grup (group - as in English)
Concert	Konser (kon-ser)
Piano	Piyano (pee-yah-no)
Guitar	Gitar (gee-tar)
Sound	Ses (ses)

Write the right words down twice on the next page

Concert	....	....
Melody	....	....
Rhythm	....	....
Sound	....	....
Guitar	....	....
Piano	....	....
Instrument	....	....
Singing	....	....
Band	....	....
Piano	....	....
Guitar	....	....
Sound	....	....
Song	....	....
Rhythm	....	....
Instrument	....	....
Singing	....	....
Band	....	....
Concert	....	....
Song	....	....
Melody	....	....

Week 3

Day 18: Jobs

Teacher	Öğretmen (oe-gret-men)
Doctor	Doktor (dok-tor)
Engineer	Mühendis (mue-hen-dis)
Chef	Şef (shef)
Police officer	Polis memuru (po-lees me-moo-roo)
Firefighter	İtfaiyeci (eet-fa-yeh-jee)
Nurse	Hemşire (hem-shee-reh)
Pilot	Pilot (pee-lot)
Lawyer	Avukat (ah-voo-kat)
Artist	Sanatçı (sah-naht-chuh)

Write the right words down twice on the next page

Lawyer	....	....
Teacher	....	....
Chef	....	....
Doctor	....	....
Engineer	....	....
Chef	....	....
Police officer	....	....
Pilot	....	....
Nurse	....	....
Doctor	....	....
Artist	....	....
Teacher	....	....
Pilot	....	....
Engineer	....	....
Artist	....	....
Police officer	....	....
Firefighter	....	....
Nurse	....	....
Lawyer	....	....
Firefighter	....	....

Week 3

Day 19: Fruits

Apple	Elma (el-mah)
Banana	Muz (mooz)
Orange	Portakal (por-tah-kal)
Strawberry	Çilek (chee-lek)
Grapes	Üzüm (ue-zoom)
Watermelon	Karpuz (kar-pooz)
Pineapple	Ananas (ah-nah-nahs)
Mango	Mango (mango - as in English)
Kiwi	Kivi (kee-vee)
Peach	Şeftali (shef-ta-lee)

Write the right words down twice on the next page

Orange	....	....
Apple	....	....
Banana	....	....
Orange	....	....
Mango	....	....
Grapes	....	....
Kiwi	....	....
Pineapple	....	....
Mango	....	....
Peach	....	....
Apple	....	....
Banana	....	....
Strawberry	....	....
Grapes	....	....
Watermelon	....	....
Pineapple	....	....
Kiwi	....	....
Strawberry	....	....
Peach	....	....
Watermelon	....	....

Week 3

Day 20: Vegetables

Carrot	Havuç (hah-vuch)
Tomato	Domates (doh-mah-tes)
Potato	Patates (pa-ta-tes)
Onion	Soğan (so-an)
Cucumber	Salatalık (sa-la-tah-luhk)
Broccoli	Brokoli (bro-ko-lee)
Spinach	Ispanak (ees-pah-nak)
Corn	Mısır (muh-suh-r)
Cabbage	Lahana (la-ha-nah)
Mushroom	Mantar (man-tar)

Write the right words down twice on the next page

Corn	....	....
Tomato	....	....
Potato	....	....
Mushroom	....	....
Spinach	....	....
Onion	....	....
Broccoli	....	....
Spinach	....	....
Corn	....	....
Tomato	....	....
Mushroom	....	....
Carrot	....	....
Cucumber	....	....
Potato	....	....
Onion	....	....
Cucumber	....	....
Cabbage	....	....
Carrot	....	....
Cabbage	....	....
Broccoli	....	....

Week 3

Day 21: Tools

Hammer	Çekiç (cheh-kich)
Screwdriver	Tornavida (tor-na-vee-dah)
Wrench	Anahtar (ah-nahk-tar)
Pliers	Pense (pen-seh)
Saw	Testere (tes-te-reh)
Drill	Matkap (maht-kahp)
Tape measure	Ölçü bandı (oe-lchew ban-duh)
Chisel	Oyma bıçağı (oy-mah buh-cha-uh)
Level	Kürek (kue-rek)
Paintbrush	Boya fırçası (bo-yah fur-cha-suh)

Write the right words down twice on the next page

Level ....

Screwdriver ....

Wrench ....

Paintbrush ....

Pliers ....

Drill ....

Chisel ....

Level ....

Paintbrush ....

Hammer ....

Screwdriver ....

Pliers ....

Saw ....

Drill ....

Tape measure ....

Hammer ....

Wrench ....

Saw ....

Chisel ....

Tape measure ....

Week 4

Day 22: Kitchen

Plate	Tabak (ta-bak)
Fork	Çatal (cha-tal)
Knife	Bıçak (buh-chahk)
Spoon	Kaşık (ka-shuhk)
Cup	Bardak (bar-dahk)
Bowl	Kase (ka-seh)
Pan	Tava (ta-vah)
Pot	Tencere (ten-je-reh)
Cutting board	Kesme tahtası (kes-meh tah-ta-suh)
Oven	Fırın (fur-un)

Write the right words down twice on the next page

Plate ....

Oven ....

Fork ....

Bowl ....

Knife ....

Spoon ....

Cup ....

Cutting board ....

Knife ....

Fork ....

Bowl ....

Spoon ....

Pan ....

Pot ....

Cutting board ....

Oven ....

Pot ....

Plate ....

Cup ....

Pan ....

Week 4

Day 23: Instruments

Guitar	Gitar (gee-tar)
Piano	Piyano (pee-yah-no)
Violin	Keman (keh-man)
Flute	Flüt (fluht)
Trumpet	Trompet (trom-pet)
Drum	Davul (dah-vool)
Saxophone	Saksafon (saks-a-fon)
Cello	Viyolonsel (vee-yo-lon-sel)
Clarinet	Klarinet (klar-i-net)
Harp	Arp (arp)

Write the right words down twice on the next page

Flute	....	....
Piano	....	....
Trumpet	....	....
Violin	....	....
Cello	....	....
Trumpet	....	....
Drum	....	....
Saxophone	....	....
Cello	....	....
Clarinet	....	....
Violin	....	....
Saxophone	....	....
Harp	....	....
Guitar	....	....
Drum	....	....
Piano	....	....
Harp	....	....
Flute	....	....
Guitar	....	....
Clarinet	....	....

Week 4

Day 24: Buildings

House	Ev (ev)
School	Okul (oh-kool)
Hospital	Hastane (has-ta-neh)
Library	Kütüphane (kue-tue-ha-neh)
Bank	Banka (ban-kah)
Restaurant	Restoran (res-to-ran)
Hotel	Otel (o-tel)
Museum	Müze (mue-ze)
Church	Kilise (kee-lee-seh)
Stadium	Stadyum (sta-dyoom)

Write the right words down twice on the next page

Hospital	....	....
House	....	....
Museum	....	....
School	....	....
Stadium	....	....
Hospital	....	....
Church	....	....
Restaurant	....	....
Hotel	....	....
Museum	....	....
Church	....	....
House	....	....
School	....	....
Library	....	....
Bank	....	....
Restaurant	....	....
Hotel	....	....
Library	....	....
Bank	....	....
Stadium	....	....

Week 4

Day 25: Directions

Left	Sol (sol)
Right	Sağ (sah)
Straight	Düz (duz)
Up	Yukarı (yoo-ka-ruh)
Down	Aşağı (a-shah-uh)
North	Kuzey (koo-zey)
South	Güney (goo-ney)
East	Doğu (do-oo)
West	Batı (ba-tee)
Stop	Dur (door)

Write the right words down twice on the next page

Straight	....	....
Left	....	....
South	....	....
Straight	....	....
Up	....	....
Down	....	....
North	....	....
Stop	....	....
East	....	....
Stop	....	....
Left	....	....
Right	....	....
South	....	....
Right	....	....
North	....	....
West	....	....
Up	....	....
Down	....	....
East	....	....
West	....	....

Week 4

Day 26: Bedroom

Bed	Yatak (ya-tahk)
Pillow	Yastık (yas-tuhk)
Blanket	Battaniye (bat-tah-nee-yeh)
Wardrobe	Gardırop (gar-duh-rop)
Nightstand	Komidin (ko-mee-deen)
Lamp	Lamba (lahm-bah)
Alarm clock	Çalar saat (cha-lar saht)
Dresser	Şifonyer (shee-fohn-yer)
Hanger	Askı (ah-skuh)
Mirror	Ayna (ah-y-nah)

Write the right words down twice on the next page

Hanger	....	....
Pillow	....	....
Dresser	....	....
Wardrobe	....	....
Mirror	....	....
Nightstand	....	....
Lamp	....	....
Alarm clock	....	....
Dresser	....	....
Blanket	....	....
Hanger	....	....
Mirror	....	....
Wardrobe	....	....
Nightstand	....	....
Bed	....	....
Blanket	....	....
Lamp	....	....
Bed	....	....
Alarm clock	....	....
Pillow	....	....

Week 4

Day 27: Countries

United States	Amerika Birleşik Devletleri (ah-meh-ree-kah beer-lesh-ik dev-let-leh-ree)
United Kingdom	Birleşik Krallık (beer-lesh-ik krahl-luhk)
Canada	Kanada (ka-nah-dah)
Australia	Avustralya (av-strahl-yah)
Germany	Almanya (al-mahn-yah)
France	Fransa (fran-sah)
China	Çin (chin)
Japan	Japonya (jah-pohn-yah)
Brazil	Brezilya (bre-zeel-yah)
India	Hindistan (hin-dis-tahn)

Write the right words down twice on the next page

China	....	....
United States	....	....
India	....	....
Canada	....	....
Australia	....	....
Brazil	....	....
China	....	....
Japan	....	....
Brazil	....	....
India	....	....
United States	....	....
Germany	....	....
Canada	....	....
Australia	....	....
Japan	....	....
United Kingdom	....	....
Germany	....	....
France	....	....
United Kingdom	....	....
France	....	....

Week 4

Day 28: Travel

Airport	Havalimanı (ha-va-lee-mah-nee)
Passport	Pasaport (pah-sah-port)
Ticket	Bilet (bee-let)
Suitcase	Bavul (bah-vool)
Hotel	Otel (oh-tel)
Sightseeing	Gezilecek yerler (geh-zil-ejek yehr-ler)
Beach	Plaj (plahj)
Adventure	Macera (mah-jeh-rah)
Map	Harita (hah-ree-tah)
Tourist	Turist (too-rist)

Write the right words down twice on the next page

Airport	....	....
Adventure	....	....
Passport	....	....
Ticket	....	....
Suitcase	....	....
Hotel	....	....
Sightseeing	....	....
Beach	....	....
Adventure	....	....
Map	....	....
Tourist	....	....
Airport	....	....
Passport	....	....
Ticket	....	....
Suitcase	....	....
Hotel	....	....
Sightseeing	....	....
Beach	....	....
Map	....	....
Tourist	....	....

Week 5

Day 29: Health

Doctor	Doktor (dohk-tor)
Hospital	Hastane (has-tah-neh)
Medicine	İlaç (ee-lahch)
Nurse	Hemşire (hem-shee-reh)
Pain	Ağrı (ah-ruh)
Appointment	Randevu (ran-deh-voo)
Exercise	Egzersiz (eg-zer-siz)
Sleep	Uyku (oo-y-koo)
Diet	Diyet (dee-yet)
Vitamin	Vitamin (vit-a-meen)

Write the right words down twice on the next page

Appointment	....	....
Vitamin	....	....
Hospital	....	....
Medicine	....	....
Nurse	....	....
Pain	....	....
Sleep	....	....
Hospital	....	....
Exercise	....	....
Nurse	....	....
Sleep	....	....
Diet	....	....
Vitamin	....	....
Doctor	....	....
Pain	....	....
Appointment	....	....
Exercise	....	....
Doctor	....	....
Medicine	....	....
Diet	....	....

Week 5

Day 30: Languages

English	İngilizce (ing-li-zjeh)
Spanish	İspanyolca (is-pahn-yol-ja)
Greek	Fransızca (fran-suhz-ja)
German	Almanca (al-man-ja)
Dutch	Hollandaca (hol-lan-da-ja)
Frisian	Frizce (freez-ja)
Russian	Rusça (roos-ja)
Portuguese	Portekizce (por-teh-kiz-ja)
Japanese	Japonca (ja-pon-ja)
Italian	İtalyanca (ee-tal-yan-ja)

Write the right words down twice on the next page

German ....

Spanish ....

Portuguese ....

Greek ....

German ....

Dutch ....

Frisian ....

Russian ....

Italian ....

Russian ....

Japanese ....

Frisian ....

English ....

Italian ....

English ....

Spanish ....

Greek ....

Dutch ....

Portuguese ....

Japanese ....

Week 5

Day 31: Church

Priest	Papaz (pah-paz)
Worship	İbadet (ee-bah-det)
Prayer	Dua (doo-ah)
Bible	Kutsal kitap (koot-sal kee-tahp)
Sermon	Vaaz (vaaz)
Choir	Koro (ko-roh)
Altar	Sunak (soo-nahk)
Cross	Haç (hach)
Faith	İman (ee-mahn)
Ceremony	Tören (toe-ren)

Write the right words down twice on the next page

Choir   ....

Worship   ....

Altar   ....

Bible   ....

Ceremony   ....

Faith   ....

Sermon   ....

Choir   ....

Altar   ....

Cross   ....

Faith   ....

Ceremony   ....

Cross   ....

Priest   ....

Worship   ....

Prayer   ....

Bible   ....

Sermon   ....

Priest   ....

Prayer   ....

Week 5

Day 32: Birds

Eagle	Kartal (kar-tal)
Sparrow	Serçe (ser-cheh)
Owl	Baykuş (bay-kush)
Parrot	Papağan (pah-pah-gahn)
Hummingbird	Sinek kuşu (see-nehk koo-shoo)
Pigeon	Güvercin (goo-ver-jin)
Flamingo	Alev kuşu (ah-lev koo-shoo)
Swan	Kuğu (koo-woo)
Peacock	Tavuskuşu (tah-voos-koo-shoo)
Duck	Ördek (oor-dehk)

Write the right words down twice on the next page

Duck	....	....
Eagle	....	....
Sparrow	....	....
Owl	....	....
Eagle	....	....
Swan	....	....
Sparrow	....	....
Flamingo	....	....
Hummingbird	....	....
Pigeon	....	....
Flamingo	....	....
Owl	....	....
Swan	....	....
Peacock	....	....
Duck	....	....
Parrot	....	....
Hummingbird	....	....
Pigeon	....	....
Parrot	....	....
Peacock	....	....

Week 5

Day 33: Science

Chemistry	Kimya (kim-yah)
Biology	Biyoloji (bee-yo-loh-jee)
Physics	Fizik (fiz-ik)
Astronomy	Astronomi (as-tro-no-mee)
Experiment	Deney (deh-ney)
Laboratory	Laboratuvar (la-bor-a-too-var)
Microscope	Mikroskop (mik-ro-skop)
Hypothesis	Hipotez (hi-po-tez)
Scientist	Bilim insanı (bee-lim in-sah-nuh)
Discovery	Keşif (keh-shif)

Write the right words down twice on the next page

Hypothesis	....	....
Biology	....	....
Experiment	....	....
Astronomy	....	....
Physics	....	....
Astronomy	....	....
Microscope	....	....
Scientist	....	....
Laboratory	....	....
Physics	....	....
Microscope	....	....
Hypothesis	....	....
Chemistry	....	....
Scientist	....	....
Discovery	....	....
Chemistry	....	....
Biology	....	....
Laboratory	....	....
Discovery	....	....
Experiment	....	....

Week 5

Day 34: Film

Actor	Oyuncu (oy-un-joo)
Actress	Oyuncu (oy-un-joo)
Director	Yönetmen (yo-net-men)
Script	Senaryo (seh-nah-ryo)
Camera	Kamera (ka-meh-rah)
Scene	Sahne (sah-ne)
Drama	Drama (drah-mah)
Comedy	Komedi (ko-meh-dee)
Action	Aksiyon (ak-si-yon)
Television	Televizyon (te-le-viz-yon)

Write the right words down twice on the next page

Actor	....	....
Camera	....	....
Action	....	....
Director	....	....
Script	....	....
Television	....	....
Camera	....	....
Scene	....	....
Drama	....	....
Comedy	....	....
Action	....	....
Television	....	....
Actor	....	....
Actress	....	....
Director	....	....
Scene	....	....
Actress	....	....
Drama	....	....
Comedy	....	....
Script	....	....

Week 5

Day 35: History

Ancient	Eski (es-kee)
Civilization	Medeniyet (meh-de-nee-yet)
Emperor	İmparator (im-par-a-tor)
Revolution	Devrim (dev-rim)
War	Savaş (sa-vahsh)
Kingdom	Krallık (kral-luhk)
Archaeology	Arkeoloji (ar-kee-oh-loh-jee)
Renaissance	Rönesans (roe-neh-sans)
Independence	Bağımsızlık (bah-uhm-suhz-luhk)
Event	Olay (o-lay)

Write the right words down twice on the next page

Kingdom	....	....
Event	....	....
Archaeology	....	....
Emperor	....	....
Renaissance	....	....
Independence	....	....
Revolution	....	....
War	....	....
Kingdom	....	....
Archaeology	....	....
Renaissance	....	....
Independence	....	....
Event	....	....
Ancient	....	....
Civilization	....	....
Emperor	....	....
Revolution	....	....
War	....	....
Ancient	....	....
Civilization	....	....

Week 6

Day 36: Drinks

Water	Su (soo)
Coffee	Kahve (kah-veh)
Tea	Çay (chay)
Juice	Meyve suyu (mey-veh soo-yoo)
Soda	Soda (so-dah)
Milk	Süt (soot)
Wine	Şarap (shah-rap)
Beer	Bira (bee-rah)
Cocktail	Kokteyl (kok-tayl)
Lemonade	Limonata (lee-mo-nah-tah)

Write the right words down twice on the next page

Soda	....	....
Cocktail	....	....
Tea	....	....
Juice	....	....
Wine	....	....
Soda	....	....
Milk	....	....
Wine	....	....
Beer	....	....
Cocktail	....	....
Lemonade	....	....
Water	....	....
Coffee	....	....
Water	....	....
Tea	....	....
Lemonade	....	....
Juice	....	....
Milk	....	....
Coffee	....	....
Beer	....	....

Week 6

Day 37: Business

Entrepreneur	Girişimci (gee-ri-shim-jee)
Company	Şirket (shir-ket)
Marketing	Pazarlama (pah-zar-lah-mah)
Sales	Satış (sa-tuhsh)
Product	Ürün (ue-roon)
Customer	Müşteri (mu-sh-teh-ree)
Finance	Finans (fee-nahns)
Strategy	Strateji (stra-teh-jee)
Profit	Kâr (kaahr)
Investment	Yatırım (yah-tuh-ruhm)

Write the right words down twice on the next page

Strategy ....

Company ....

Marketing ....

Sales ....

Product ....

Customer ....

Finance ....

Investment ....

Customer ....

Profit ....

Finance ....

Investment ....

Entrepreneur ....

Company ....

Marketing ....

Sales ....

Product ....

Profit ....

Entrepreneur ....

Strategy ....

Week 6

Day 38: Beach

Sand	Kum (koom)
Waves	Dalga (dal-gah)
Sunscreen	Güneş kremi (goo-nesh kre-mee)
Swim	Yüzme (yuz-meh)
Seashells	Deniz kabukları (deh-niz ka-book-lah-ruh)
Umbrella	Şemsiye (shem-si-yeh)
Beach ball	Plaj topu (plahj toh-poo)
Sunbathing	Güneşlenme (goo-nesh-len-meh)
Surfing	Sörf (surf)
Picnic	Piknik (pick-nick)

Write the right words down twice on the next page

Beach ball	....	....
Sunbathing	....	....
Waves	....	....
Sunscreen	....	....
Picnic	....	....
Swim	....	....
Umbrella	....	....
Beach ball	....	....
Picnic	....	....
Sand	....	....
Sunscreen	....	....
Swim	....	....
Seashells	....	....
Surfing	....	....
Waves	....	....
Umbrella	....	....
Seashells	....	....
Sunbathing	....	....
Surfing	....	....
Sand	....	....

Week 6

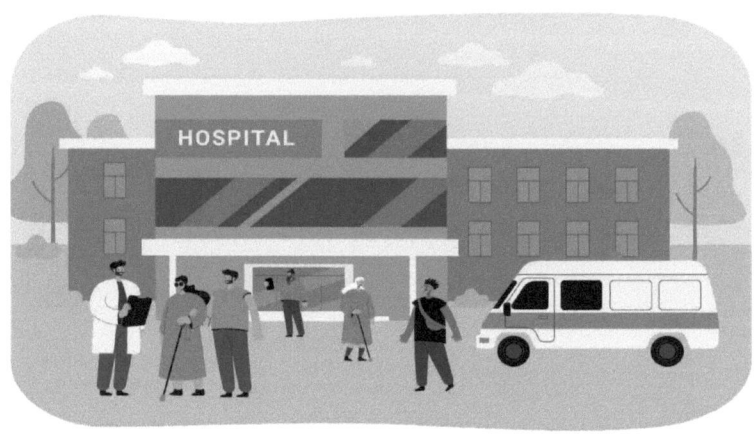

Day 39: Hospital

Doctor	Doktor (dohk-tor)
Nurse	Hemşire (hem-shee-reh)
Patient	Hasta (has-tah)
Emergency	Acil durum (ah-jil doo-room)
Surgery	Cerrahi (jer-ra-hee)
Appointment	Randevu (ran-deh-voo)
Stethoscope	Stetoskop (stet-os-kop)
X-ray	Röntgen (ront-gen)
Medicine	İlaç (ee-lahch)
Recovery	İyileşme (ee-yi-lesh-meh)

Write the right words down twice on the next page

Nurse	....	....
Doctor	....	....
Appointment	....	....
Stethoscope	....	....
Emergency	....	....
Recovery	....	....
Nurse	....	....
Patient	....	....
Emergency	....	....
Surgery	....	....
Appointment	....	....
Stethoscope	....	....
X-ray	....	....
Medicine	....	....
Recovery	....	....
Doctor	....	....
Surgery	....	....
Patient	....	....
X-ray	....	....
Medicine	....	....

Week 6

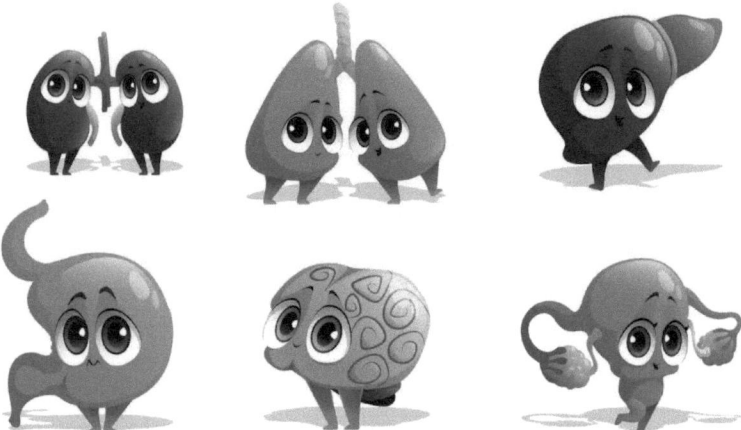

Day 40: Internal Body

Heart   Kalp (kahlp)

Lungs   Akciğerler (ahk-jee-yehr-lehr)

Stomach   Mide (mee-deh)

Liver   Karaciğer (kah-rah-jee-yehr)

Kidneys   Böbrekler (buh-brek-lerr)

Brain   Beyin (bey-in)

Intestines   Bağırsaklar (bah-uh-rsahk-lahr)

Bladder   Mesane (meh-sah-neh)

Bones   Kemikler (keh-mik-lerr)

Muscles   Kaslar (kahs-lahr)

Write the right words down twice on the next page

Kidneys	....	....
Stomach	....	....
Heart	....	....
Intestines	....	....
Brain	....	....
Lungs	....	....
Stomach	....	....
Liver	....	....
Muscles	....	....
Kidneys	....	....
Intestines	....	....
Bladder	....	....
Bones	....	....
Muscles	....	....
Heart	....	....
Lungs	....	....
Bones	....	....
Liver	....	....
Brain	....	....
Bladder	....	....

Week 6

Day 41: Internet

Website	Web sitesi (web site-see)
Email	E-posta (e-pos-tah)
Social media	Sosyal medya (soh-syal med-yah)
Online shopping	Online alışveriş (on-line ah-luhsh-veh-reesh)
Search engine	Arama motoru (ah-rah-mah moh-toh-roo)
Password	Parola (pah-roh-lah)
Wi-Fi	Wi-Fi (wee-fee)
Download	İndirme (een-deer-meh)
Upload	Yükleme (yook-leh-meh)
Browser	Tarayıcı (tah-ry-uh-jee)

Write the right words down twice on the next page

Browser	....	....
Website	....	....
Email	....	....
Social media	....	....
Wi-Fi	....	....
Search engine	....	....
Password	....	....
Wi-Fi	....	....
Download	....	....
Upload	....	....
Browser	....	....
Online shopping	....	....
Email	....	....
Social media	....	....
Online shopping	....	....
Password	....	....
Website	....	....
Download	....	....
Upload	....	....
Search engine	....	....

Week 6

Day 42: Shapes

Cirkel	Daire (dahy-reh)
Square	Kare (kah-reh)
Rectangle	Dikdörtgen (dik-duhrt-gen)
Triangle	Üçgen (ooch-gen)
Oval	Oval (oh-val)
Pyramid	Piramit (pee-rah-mit)
Cube	Küp (kuep)
Arrow	Ok (ohk)
Star	Yıldız (yuhl-duhz)
Cylinder	Silindir (see-lin-deer)

Write the right words down twice on the next page

Rectangle	....	....
Triangle	....	....
Pyramid	....	....
Arrow	....	....
Star	....	....
Cylinder	....	....
Oval	....	....
Square	....	....
Star	....	....
Cube	....	....
Cirkel	....	....
Pyramid	....	....
Cylinder	....	....
Cirkel	....	....
Square	....	....
Rectangle	....	....
Triangle	....	....
Oval	....	....
Cube	....	....
Arrow	....	....

Week 7

Day 43: House Parts

Roof	Çatı (cha-tuh)
Door	Kapı (kah-pee)
Window	Pencere (pen-jeh-reh)
Floor	Zemin (zeh-min)
Wall	Duvar (doo-var)
Ceiling	Tavan (tah-vahn)
Stairs	Merdivenler (mer-dee-ven-lerr)
Bathroom	Banyo (ban-yoh)
Kitchen	Mutfak (moot-fahk)
Bedroom	Yatak odası (yah-tahk oh-dah-suh)

Write the right words down twice on the next page

Wall	....	....
Door	....	....
Stairs	....	....
Ceiling	....	....
Floor	....	....
Wall	....	....
Ceiling	....	....
Bedroom	....	....
Stairs	....	....
Bathroom	....	....
Kitchen	....	....
Bedroom	....	....
Roof	....	....
Door	....	....
Window	....	....
Floor	....	....
Roof	....	....
Bathroom	....	....
Kitchen	....	....
Window	....	....

Week 7

Day 44: Around the House

Plant	Bitki (bit-kee)
Watering can	Sulama kabı (soo-lah-mah kah-buh)
Shed	Kulübe (koo-loo-beh)
Doorbell	Kapı zili (kah-pee zee-lee)
Fence	Çit (chit)
Mailbox	Posta kutusu (pos-tah koo-too-soo)
Lawn mower	Çim biçme makinesi (chim bich-meh mah-kee-neh-see)
Wheelbarrow	El arabası (el ah-rah-bah-suh)
Shovel	Kürek (kue-rek)
Bench	Bank (bank)

Write the right words down twice on the next page

Watering can ....

Shed ....

Doorbell ....

Mailbox ....

Bench ....

Fence ....

Wheelbarrow ....

Shed ....

Mailbox ....

Bench ....

Lawn mower ....

Wheelbarrow ....

Shovel ....

Plant ....

Watering can ....

Doorbell ....

Fence ....

Lawn mower ....

Shovel ....

Plant ....

Week 7

Day 45: Face

Eyes	Gözler (goz-lerr)
Nose	Burun (boo-run)
Mouth	Ağız (ah-uhz)
Ears	Kulaklar (koo-lahk-lahr)
Cheeks	Yanaklar (yah-nahk-lahr)
Forehead	Alın (ah-luhn)
Chin	Çene (cheh-neh)
Lips	Dudaklar (doo-dahk-lahr)
Teeth	Dişler (dish-lerr)
Eyebrows	Kaşlar (kash-lahr)

Write the right words down twice on the next page

Eyebrows	....	....
Nose	....	....
Chin	....	....
Forehead	....	....
Ears	....	....
Cheeks	....	....
Forehead	....	....
Chin	....	....
Nose	....	....
Lips	....	....
Teeth	....	....
Eyebrows	....	....
Eyes	....	....
Lips	....	....
Teeth	....	....
Mouth	....	....
Ears	....	....
Mouth	....	....
Cheeks	....	....
Eyes	....	....

Week 7

Day 46: Bathroom

Sink   Lavabo (lah-vah-boh)

Toilet   Tuvalet (too-vah-let)

Shower   Duş (doosh)

Bathtub   Küvet (kue-vet)

Mirror   Ayna (ai-nah)

Towel   Havlu (hav-loo)

Soap   Sabun (sah-boon)

Toothbrush   Diş fırçası (dish fur-shah-suh)

Shampoo   Şampuan (shahm-pwan)

Hairdryer   Saç kurutma makinesi (sahch koo-root-mah mah-kee-neh-see)

Write the right words down twice on the next page

Mirror	....	....
Sink	....	....
Hairdryer	....	....
Shower	....	....
Bathtub	....	....
Mirror	....	....
Towel	....	....
Soap	....	....
Toothbrush	....	....
Toilet	....	....
Shampoo	....	....
Towel	....	....
Soap	....	....
Hairdryer	....	....
Sink	....	....
Toilet	....	....
Shower	....	....
Bathtub	....	....
Toothbrush	....	....
Shampoo	....	....

Week 7

Day 47: Living Room

Sofa	Kanepe (kah-neh-peh)
Television	Televizyon (tel-ev-iz-yon)
Coffee table	Sehpa (seh-pah)
Bookshelf	Kitaplık (kee-tahp-likh)
Lamp	Lamba (lahm-bah)
Rug	Halı (hal-uh)
Cushion	Yastık (yas-tuhk)
Remote control	Uzaktan kumanda (oo-zak-tahn koo-mahn-dah)
Curtains	Perdeler (per-deh-lerr)
Fireplace	Şömine (shoh-mee-neh)

Write the right words down twice on the next page

Rug	....	....
Sofa	....	....
Remote control	....	....
Television	....	....
Coffee table	....	....
Bookshelf	....	....
Lamp	....	....
Cushion	....	....
Curtains	....	....
Fireplace	....	....
Sofa	....	....
Television	....	....
Fireplace	....	....
Lamp	....	....
Rug	....	....
Cushion	....	....
Remote control	....	....
Curtains	....	....
Bookshelf	....	....
Coffee table	....	....

Week 7

Day 48: Finance

Budget	Bütçe (boot-cheh)
Savings	Tasarruflar (tah-sar-roo-flar)
Debt	Borç (borch)
Income	Gelir (geh-lir)
Expenses	Giderler (gee-der-lerr)
Bank account	Banka hesabı (bank-ah he-sah-buh)
Credit card	Kredi kartı (kred-ee kart-uh)
Interest	Faiz (fah-iz)
Loan	Kredi (kred-ee)
Stock market	Hisse senedi piyasası (his-seh seh-neh-dee pyah-sah-suh)

Write the right words down twice on the next page

Savings	....	....
Loan	....	....
Debt	....	....
Income	....	....
Expenses	....	....
Budget	....	....
Income	....	....
Expenses	....	....
Interest	....	....
Loan	....	....
Stock market	....	....
Budget	....	....
Bank account	....	....
Credit card	....	....
Debt	....	....
Savings	....	....
Interest	....	....
Bank account	....	....
Credit card	....	....
Stock market	....	....

Week 7

Day 49: Books

Writer	Yazar (yah-zahr)
Page	Sayfa (say-fah)
Table of Contents	İçindekiler (ee-chin-deh-kee-lerr)
Foreword	Önsöz (ohn-soz)
Introduction	Giriş (gee-reesh)
Front cover	Ön kapak (ohn kah-pahk)
Back cover	Arka kapak (ahr-kah kah-pahk)
Text	Metin (meh-tin)
Title	Başlık (bash-luhk)
Picture	Resim (reh-seem)

Write the right words down twice on the next page

Front cover

Table of Contents

Title

Picture

Introduction

Back cover

Page

Foreword

Title

Text

Back cover

Picture

Writer

Page

Table of Contents

Foreword

Introduction

Front cover

Writer

Text

Week 8

Day 50: Law

Witness	Tanık (tah-nuhk)
Justice	Adalet (ah-dah-let)
Judge	Hakim (hah-kim)
Victim	Mağdur (mah-dur)
Perpetrator	Suçlu (sooch-loo)
Court	Mahkeme (mah-keh-meh)
Evidence	Delil (deh-lil)
Lawyer	Avukat (ah-voo-kat)
Crime	Suç (sooch)
Government	Hükümet (huhk-oo-met)

Write the right words down twice on the next page

Perpetrator ....

Court ....

Justice ....

Evidence ....

Victim ....

Government ....

Judge ....

Victim ....

Perpetrator ....

Court ....

Evidence ....

Lawyer ....

Crime ....

Government ....

Witness ....

Justice ....

Crime ....

Judge ....

Witness ....

Lawyer ....

Help Us Share Your Thoughts!

Dear Reader,

Thank you for choosing to read our book. We hope you enjoyed the journey through its pages and that it left a positive impact on your life. As an independent author, reviews from readers like you are incredibly valuable in helping us reach a wider audience and improve our craft.

If you enjoyed our book, we kindly ask for a moment of your time to leave an honest review. Your feedback can make a world of difference by providing potential readers with insight into the book's content and your personal experience.

Your review doesn't have to be lengthy or complicated—just a few lines expressing your genuine thoughts would be immensely appreciated. We value your feedback and take it to heart, using it to shape our future work and create more content that resonates with readers like you.

By leaving a review, you are not only supporting us as authors but also helping other readers discover this book. Your voice matters, and your words have the power to inspire others to embark on this literary journey.

We genuinely appreciate your time and willingness to share your thoughts. Thank you for being an essential part of our author journey.